"If they can
dream it, they
can build it."
—MADHU THANGAVELU

For Scott and Kate—may you always keep dreaming up

dreaming UP

a celebration of building

UP

Christy Hale

Lee & Low Books Inc.   New York

Cup
on cup
stacking up,
smaller, smaller,
and growing taller!

Earth and water, sun and air, all around, everywhere!

Cold and wet, hot and dry, mixed together—make mud pie.

Open the top   and in I hop,

poke out a square to see who's there,

pull in the flap to hide from view—

Can you see me? *I see you!*

Blankets flung, stretched chair to chair—soft roof arcs low.

A cozy place, a hideaway,
where you and I can go.

Touch
wood.
Fingers learn each form.
Hang shapes on
air,
explore new directions.
Every
block
anchored with care.

Fluid
with
water,

Towers
twist
high,

Sparkle
with
sea glass,

treasures,
and
shells.

sand castle

One by one,
block by block,
plastic shapes
interlock.

Yellow, **red**,
white, and **black**,
all connect
in a stack.

Build a world
brick by brick.
Hold them close.
Hear the *click*.

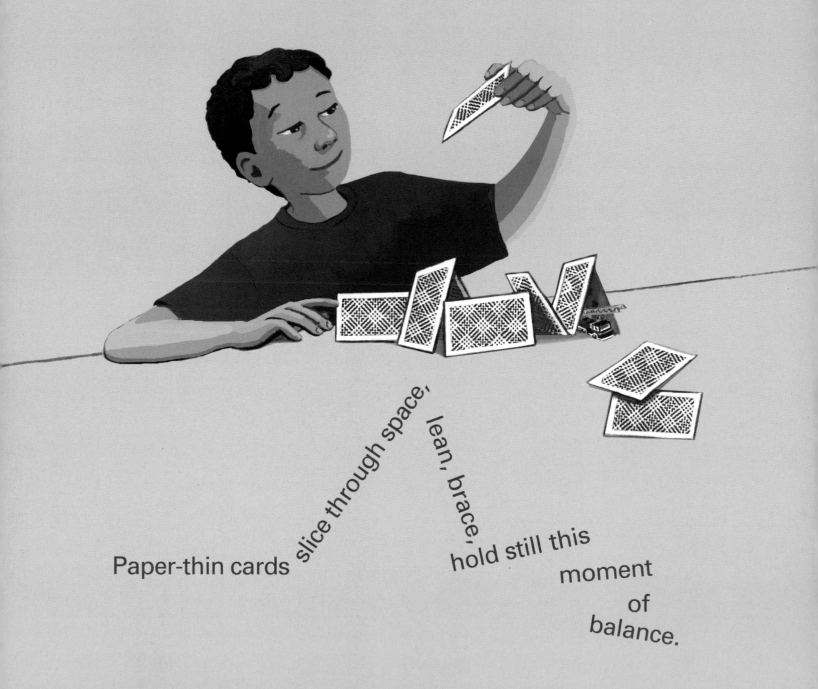

Paper-thin cards slice through space, lean, brace, hold still this moment of balance.

Easy peasy as can be toothpicks joining

• ONE •

• TWO • THREE •

Sticks touch like fingertips——reach high where wishes roam.

Cupped between is magic space

in a forest fairy home.

Balls of snow, ground.

bags of land, built on

bend down low, home is,

fill your hand. Dome is,

Pack them, circle round.

stack them,

Paper tubes, stuff reused, anything does the trick. Tape or glue **for** strength, **and** **you** have raised a building quick!

flat wooden sticks stuck with glue
gaps in between where sun peeks through
solid then open, dark then bright
shifting patterns, flickering light
slats and slits standing side by side
add together, build round and wide

an open floor
inviting space
welcome door
to Popsicle Place

add together, build round and wide
slats and slits standing side by side
shifting patterns, flickering light
solid then open, dark then bright,
gaps in between where sun peeks through
flat wooden sticks stuck with glue

Soft tumble forms making ever-changing caverns, secret spaces, pillow forts

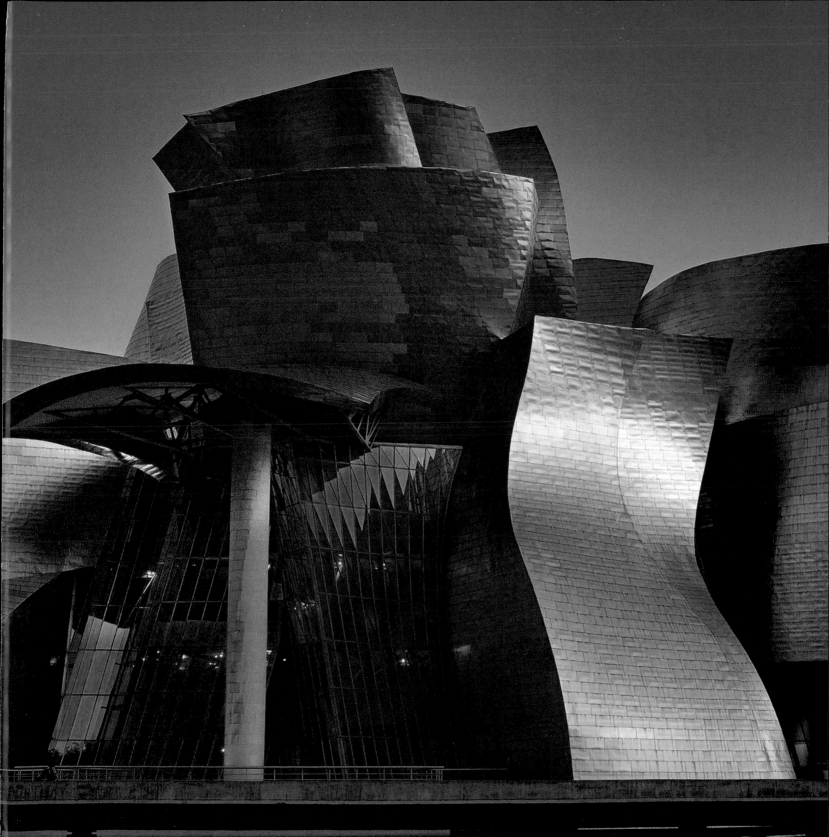

SOLOMON R. GUGGENHEIM MUSEUM

NEW YORK, NEW YORK, USA, 1959
Like upside-down stacking rings, this concrete building is wider at the top than at the bottom. Visitors start at the upper level and view art in a continuous stroll down a spiral ramp.

FRANK LLOYD WRIGHT

(b. 1867 in Richland Center, Wisconsin; d. 1959) See FALLINGWATER, another building designed by Frank Lloyd Wright, to learn about the architect.

"That early kindergarten experience with the straight line; the flat plane; the square; the triangle; the circle! . . .
These primary forms and figures were the secret of all effects . . . which were ever got into the architecture of the world."

PETRONAS TWIN TOWERS

KUALA LUMPUR, MALAYSIA, 1998
These two towers taper like graduated cups as they climb higher and higher. Built from concrete, steel, and glass, they were the world's tallest buildings from 1998 to 2004.

CÉSAR PELLI

(b. 1926 in San Miguel de Tucumán, Argentina–) spent many childhood hours reading books from his family's large library. He liked books with pictures best. Pelli also loved to draw and construct bridges, forts, and towers. West of his family's home, the Andes filled the sky. This imposing range became his ever-present inspiration. Pelli studied to become an architect and went on to design some of the world's tallest structures. His buildings rise up like the mountains.

"The desire to reach for the sky runs deep in our human psyche."

NEW GOURNA VILLAGE

NEAR LUXOR, EGYPT, 1948
Four basic elements (earth, water, sun, air), traditional design methods, sensitivity to the climate, and imagination were combined to make this earthen village.

HASSAN FATHY

(b. 1900 in Alexandria, Egypt; d. 1989) listened to his mother's stories of her youth in the country, where self-sufficient people produced whatever they needed to live; and he dreamed of creating his own ideal village. Fathy became a pioneer of sustainable building and was devoted to housing the poor. For New Gourna Village, he trained local villagers to make their own materials and construct their houses and other buildings. The World Monuments Fund has worked to promote the preservation of New Gourna's architectural heritage.

"The human spirit is our most precious resource."

BOX HOUSE

TELLURIDE, COLORADO, USA, 2006
When at home, residents open out the slatted screens, welcoming in light and the Rocky Mountain setting. When they leave, they pull the shutters back in, closing up the house like a simple wooden box.

MAYA LIN

(b. 1959 in Athens, Ohio–) often played alone as a child, exploring the woods near home or building miniature worlds in her room. Lin's parents worked at Ohio University. Her mother was a poet and professor of literature, and her father was a ceramics teacher and dean of the fine arts department. Lin enjoyed sculpting objects in her father's studio. Her Chinese heritage and love of play unite in the Box House. Asian puzzle boxes with hidden panels, secret sliding doors, and opening parts inspired her design.

"The process I go through in art and architecture, I actually want it to be almost childlike. Sometimes I think it's magical."

YOYOGI NATIONAL STADIUM TOKYO, JAPAN, 1964

The shape and texture of this modern building were inspired by traditional Japanese temples and farmhouses. The stadium is world famous for its suspension roof, which curves over the top like draped fabric.

KENZO TANGE (b. 1913 in Osaka, Japan; d. 2005) was skilled in math as a child and planned to become an astronomer. One day he noticed some drawings in a magazine by the architect Le Corbusier, which sparked his own interest in architecture. Tange's work, spare and elegant, expressed his knowledge of past Japanese structures and culture combined with new ideas from the West. Yoyogi National Stadium, designed for the 1964 Tokyo Olympics, is often described as one of the most beautiful structures built in the twentieth century.

"Architecture must have something that appeals to the human heart."

FALLINGWATER

BEAR RUN, PENNSYLVANIA, USA, 1939

Although weighted into the hillside by a large stone chimney, the house appears to float above the ground. The building becomes part of the landscape. Concrete slab balconies and terraces extend over a waterfall and stream below.

FRANK LLOYD WRIGHT (b. 1867 in Richland Center, Wisconsin; d. 1959) was destined to be an architect. His mother planned this future for him before he was born. She bought him maple wood blocks, and he played with them for hours, developing a strong sense of geometry and three-dimensional forms. Wright loved nature and wanted people to live in harmony with their surroundings. He designed unique buildings for more than seventy years—changing, adapting, using the latest materials and engineering, yet always respecting the setting and environment.

"The maple wood blocks . . . are in my fingers to this day."

LA SAGRADA FAMÍLIA

BARCELONA, SPAIN, 1883–

In this grand basilica, exuberant sculpted towers point to the sky. The crowns of the spires are covered in mosaics made from pieces of different-colored glass. The basilica, still under construction, is Gaudí's unfinished masterpiece.

ANTONI GAUDÍ (b. 1852 in Reus, Spain; d. 1926) suffered early in life from rheumatic fever, which made walking painful and prevented him from playing with other children. He spent his days alone observing animals, plants, and stones. When Gaudí became an architect, he designed whimsical structures that swirled and flowed. He was an early recycler, incorporating discarded ceramic shards into playful mosaics. The shapes, textures, and decorative colors in Gaudí's work, unlike anything seen before, were inspired by forms he found in the natural world.

"There are no straight lines or sharp corners in nature."

HABITAT 67

MONTRÉAL, QUÉBEC, CANADA, 1967

This housing complex provides affordable living spaces made of modular stacking units arranged in various combinations. Although the homes are close together, each has a garden terrace. The homes unite to form a gigantic urban sculpture.

MOSHE SAFDIE (b. 1937 in Haifa, Israel–) grew up in Haifa, a city on a hill. The family also spent summers on communal farms, where young Safdie worked among many others. When he was fifteen, the family moved to Canada, and Safdie later studied architecture at McGill University. Safdie's memories of Haifa's hillside dwellings and his sense of community, developed on the farms, inspired his thesis project at McGill: a modular building system constructed from LEGO blocks. Habitat 67, built for Canada's Expo 67, developed from his thesis explorations.

"I want my children to be able to meet and play and communicate with many other children on their own."

VITRA FIRE STATION

WEIL AM RHEIN, GERMANY, 1994

When the alarm rang in this fire station, firefighters burst into action. The building, with its sharp, tilted planes, appears ready to explode into action too. Doors slid open. Red engines roared to the fire.

ZAHA HADID (b. 1950 in

Baghdad, Iraq–) grew up during a progressive period of Iraq's history. She was well educated and encouraged to think freely. Her father's best friend designed a house for Hadid's aunt. The architectural model—it looked almost like a dollhouse—fascinated the young girl and sparked her interest in architecture. Hadid's buildings are dynamic, innovative structures that often seem to fly through the air, breaking the rules of gravity. The Vitra Fire Station, her first completed project, looks like the wing of a bird.

"In every project there are new territories to be invented and to be conquered."

MONTRÉAL BIOSPHÈRE

MONTRÉAL, QUÉBEC, CANADA, 1967

Triangles made of metal tubes join together to form this huge sphere called a geodesic dome. The structure is as tall as a twenty-story building.

R. BUCKMINSTER FULLER

(b. 1895 in Milton, Massachusetts; d. 1983) was born with poor eyesight. When he was prescribed eyeglasses at age four, he began to see the details of nature and the changing world around him. Fuller was a visionary thinker and problem solver. His ideas became inventions designed to use the fewest natural resources while benefiting the greatest number of people. Geodesic domes are lightweight and sturdy. They can be built to any size without supports inside, and they become proportionally lighter and stronger as they increase in size. Originally the U.S. Pavilion at Expo 67, the Biosphère now houses an environmental museum.

"[Children] spontaneously experiment and experience. . . . They select, combine, and test, seeking to find order in their experiences."

BAMBOO CHURCH

CARTAGENA, COLOMBIA, 2007

This open-air church looks like the nave of a Gothic cathedral. The architect's inspiration came from bamboo forests, where the branches of trees bend toward one another to create a high-peaked arch.

SIMÓN VÉLEZ (b. 1949 in Manizales,

Colombia–) is from a family of builders. Both his father and grandfather were architects who worked with standard materials. Vélez tried new things. He noticed that simple bamboo buildings withstood earthquakes, while more expensive concrete structures crumbled. Bamboo is stronger and more flexible than steel, and it is the fastest-growing plant on Earth—a great renewable resource. Vélez developed ways to use bamboo in modern building, and for decades he has engineered many temporary and permanent bamboo structures.

"Bamboo is the green steel of nature."

MARS ONE

HESPERIA, CALIFORNIA, USA, 1998

This sample shelter for living on Mars rises from a circular base. Sandbags filled with soil are stacked into a dome-like shape and held together with Velcro. The dome is strong enough to withstand a Martian windstorm.

NADER KHALILI (b. 1936 in

Tehran, Iran; d. 2008) was one of nine children in a poor family. He studied engineering and architecture in Turkey and the United States. After a successful career building high-rises, Khalili turned his attention to helping the hundreds of millions of people in the world who had unsuitable housing. He taught refugees, disaster victims, and the poor to build simple houses using the earth beneath their feet. Khalili believed that on Mars, and on the moon too, the best substances for constructing shelters would be the materials under the astronauts' feet.

"Everything we need to build is in us, and in the place."

PAPER TUBE SCHOOL

CHENGDU, SICHUAN, CHINA, 2008
Teachers and students helped construct this temporary school out of plywood and recycled heavy-duty paper tubes after an earthquake destroyed many buildings in China's Sichuan Province.

SHIGERU BAN (b. 1957 in Tokyo, Japan–) grew up wanting to travel like his fashion designer mother, who returned from each trip with fascinating souvenirs of the world beyond Japan. Ban studied architecture in Los Angeles and New York. He has since become famous for his innovative emergency and permanent structures. Ban finds new ways to recycle materials, making the most out of whatever is available. Beverage crates, shipping containers, cardboard tubes, and even old tea bags have been used in his buildings.

"Anything can be building structure material."

SCLERA PAVILION

LONDON, ENGLAND, 2008
Vertical slats of wood were used to create this circular building. The open design allowed for a shifting play of light and shadow that changed people's experience of the space as they walked through the pavilion.

DAVID ADJAYE (b.1966 in Dar es Salaam, Tanzania–) is the son of a Ghanaian diplomat. The family lived throughout Africa until they settled in Britain when Adjaye was nine. His disabled brother was placed in a care facility. The depressing environment there inspired Adjaye to become an architect and create spaces that would lift the spirit. He has often collaborated with artists and is known for his colorful, eclectic designs and for working with timber. Adjaye's buildings blend simple forms with abstract rhythms and reflect patterns of African textiles.

"Space is created from lights and shadow. . . . It needs you—your eyes, your mind—to fill it."

GUGGENHEIM MUSEUM BILBAO
BILBAO, SPAIN, 1997
Located on a river, this limestone, glass, and textured titanium building gives the impression of a fish or a ship in the water. The curves and angles add movement and feeling to the structure.

FRANK GEHRY (b.1929 in Toronto, Canada–) would sit on the floor as a child arranging wood scraps into little cities and freeways. He later studied architecture at the University of Southern California. Gehry always loved to draw, and all his designs begin as loose, freestyle sketches. His buildings often include eccentric shapes but are designed with a concern for how people move through them and with sensitivity to the environment. The Guggenheim Museum Bilbao is considered to be one of the most significant architectural works of the late twentieth century.

"Creativity is about play and a kind of willingness to go with your intuition."

ACKNOWLEDGMENTS
I am grateful to architect Catharine Fergus Garber of Fergus Garber Young Architects; my Lewis & Clark College art history professor, Stewart Buettner; Kara Adams; poets Gail Newman and Caroline Goodwin; my writers group: Debbie Duncan, Kirk Glaser, Heidi R. Kling, Cynthia Chin-Lee, Kevin Kiser, SuAnn Kiser, and Mark Reibstein; and my illustrators group: Ashley Wolff, Julie Downing, Lisa Brown, and Katherine Tillotson, for their many helpful suggestions. Thanks to Wing Cheng and Ivan Onatra for help in translating and contacting photographers and architects. A special thank-you to my editor, Louise May, for her support, suggestions, and careful attention to all details. Thanks to all of my Lee & Low family for giving me yet another opportunity to keep "dreaming up."

PHOTOGRAPH CREDITS
Solomon R. Guggenheim Museum: © 1994–2009 Scott Gilchrist/Archivision Inc.; Petronas Twin Towers: © Brand X Pictures/www.fotosearch.com; New Gourna Village: © World Monuments Fund; Box House: © Paul Warchol; Yoyogi National Stadium: Photograph by Osamu Murai; Fallingwater: Robert P. Ruschak, courtesy of the Western Pennsylvania Conservancy; La Sagrada Família: © Purestock/Glow Images; Habitat 67: © Jeffrey M. Frank/Shutterstock.com; Vitra Fire Station: © Christian Richters; Montréal Biosphère: © delkoo/depositphotos; Bamboo Church: © Hitesh Mehta; Mars One: Courtesy of Cal-Earth, The California Institute of Earth Art and Architecture; Paper Tube School: © Tao Zhu; Sclera Pavilion: Photograph by Johnny Boylan, sponsored by AHEC; Guggenheim Museum Bilbao: FREE stock Photos #628

FSC
MIX
Paper from responsible sources
www.fsc.org   FSC® C109093

AUTHOR'S SOURCES

Frank Lloyd Wright

Hoffmann, Donald. *Frank Lloyd Wright's Fallingwater: The House and Its History.* New York: Dover, 1978.

"Influence of Friedrich Froebel: Frank Lloyd Wright." Froebel Web. http://www.froebelweb.org/web2000.html.

Kaufmann, Edgar Jr. *Fallingwater: A Frank Lloyd Wright Country House.* New York: Abbeville Press, 1986.

Starita, Angela. "Keeping Faith with an Idea: A Timeline of the Guggenheim Museum, 1943–1959." http://web.guggenheim.org/timeline/index.html. Adapted from Hilary Ballon, et al. *The Guggenheim: Frank Lloyd Wright and the Making of the Modern Museum.* New York: Guggenheim Museum, 2009.

Waggoner, Lynda, ed. *Fallingwater.* New York: Rizzoli, 2011.

Wright, Frank Lloyd. *An Autobiography.* New York: Horizon Press, 1977.

César Pelli

Hoffman, Nicholas von. "Cesar Pelli: Creating an architecture that is responsive to function and place." *Architectural Digest* 62, issue 3 (March 2005): 74.

"MegaStructures: Petronas Towers." Spike: National Geographic Channel online. http://www.spike.com/video-clips/b1io0j/national-geographic-channel-megastructures-petronas-towers-petronas-towers.

Hassan Fathy

Dethier, Jean. *Down to Earth: Adobe Architecture: An Old Idea, a New Future.* New York: Facts on File, 1983.

Fathy, Hassan. *Architecture for the Poor: An Experiment in Rural Egypt.* Chicago: University of Chicago Press, 1973.

Maya Lin

Lashnits, Tom. *Maya Lin.* New York: Chelsea House, 2007.

Maya Lin: A Strong Clear Vision. Directed by Freida Lee Mock. New York: New Video Group. Released May 27, 2003. DVD, 105 min.

Kenzo Tange

Drew, Philip. *Tensile Architecture.* Boulder, CO: Westview Press, 1979.

"Kenzo Tange." *The Telegraph,* March 23, 2005. Obituaries. http://www.telegraph.co.uk/news/obituaries/1486218/Kenzo-Tange.html.

Antoni Gaudí

Antonio Gaudí. Directed by Hiroshi Teshigahara. New York: Criterion Collection. Released March 18, 2008. DVD, 72 min.

Descharnes, Robert, and Clovis Prevost. *Gaudí: The Visionary.* New York: Viking Press, 1971.

Hensbergen, Gijs van. *Gaudí: A Biography.* New York: HarperCollins, 2001.

Moshe Safdie

Bergdoll, Barry, and Peter Christensen. *Home Delivery: Fabricating the Modern Dwelling.* New York: Museum of Modern Art, 2008.

"Little Boxes: Moshe Safdie's Habitat '67." CBC/Radio-Canada Digital Archives. Online video of program broadcast February 3, 1966. http://www.cbc.ca/archives/categories/arts-entertainment/architecture/moshe-safdie-hero-of-habitat/little-boxes-habitat-67.html.

"Moshe Safdie: Israeli Roots." CBC/Radio-Canada Digital Archives. Online video of program broadcast March 16, 1971. http://www.cbc.ca/archives/categories/arts-entertainment/architecture/moshe-safdie-hero-of-habitat/israeli-roots.html.

"Moshe Safdie on Habitat '67." CBC/Radio-Canada Digital Archives. Online video of program broadcast October 25,1966.http://www.cbc.ca/archives/categories/arts-entertainment/architecture/moshe-safdie-hero-of-habitat/moshe-safdie-on-habitat-67.html.

Wachtel, Eleanor. "Moshe Safdie architect." *Queen's Quarterly,* June 22, 2008: 199–201.

Zaha Hadid

Mertins, Detlef, Patrik Schumacher, and Joseph Giovannini. *Zaha Hadid Exhibition Catalogue.* New York: Guggenheim Museum, 2006.

Pearman, Hugh. "Iraqitect: Zaha Hadid commands the Guggenheim, but remembers her roots." *The London Sunday Times Magazine,* June 4, 2006. http://www.hughpearman.com/2006/17.html.

R. Buckminster Fuller

Aaseng, Nathan. *More with Less: The Future World of Buckminster Fuller.* Minneapolis, MN: Lerner Publications, 1986.

Buckminster Fuller Institute: http://bfi.org/.

Building Big: Domes. Directed by Tom Levenson. PBS/WGBH Boston. Released October 26, 2004. DVD, 63 min.

Simón Vélez

Drost, Nadja. "Bamboo Architect Simon Velez." Produced by Global Post, 2010. http://www.dailymotion.com/video/xl16h5_bamboo-architect-simon-velez_news.

Goris, Gie, and Wouter Tordoor, trans. "Colombian top architect Simón Vélez calls for buildings on a human scale." *MO Mondiaal Nieuws,* March 24, 2010. http://www.mo.be/node/149034.

Katakam, Ramu. "An enduring love affair with bamboo." *Frontline* 27, issue 15 (July 17–30, 2010).

Vélez, Simón. *Grow Your Own House: Simón Vélez and Bamboo Architecture.* Weil am Rhein, Germany: Vitra Design Museum, 2000.

Nader Khalili

Khalili, Nader. "Magma, Ceramic, and Fused Adobe Structures Generated In-Situ." In *Lunar Bases and Space Activities of the 21st Century,* edited by W. W. Mendell, 399–404. Houston, TX: Lunar and Planetary Institute, 1985.

Thangavelu, Madhu. "Lunar and Terrestrial Sustainable Building Technology in the New Millennium: An Interview with Architect Nader Khalili." *Building Standards,* January–February, 2000: 44–47.

Shigeru Ban

Architecture for Humanity. *Design Like You Give a Damn: Architectural Responses to Humanitarian Crises.* New York: Metropolis Books, 2006.

Benhamou-Huet, Judith. "Shigeru Ban." *Interview Magazine,* April 28, 2009. http://www.interviewmagazine.com/art/shigeru-ban/.

Pasternack, Alex. "An Earthquake-Ready School for China (Just Add Cardboard Tubes)." Treehugger, January 7, 2009. http://current.com/1ft7a4c.

David Adjaye

American Hardwood Export Council. *Sclera, full edit.* Narrated by David Venables. Vimeo. Online video. http://vimeo.com/1988549.

David Adjaye: Bus Shelter. Super Contemporary Exhibition, Design Museum and Beefeater 24. http://www.supercontemporary.co.uk/index.php?s=david-adjaye.

Scaro, Diego Garcia. Interview with David Adjaye. *IconEye: Icon Magazine Online.* http://www.iconeye.com/news/david-adjaye.

Frank Gehry

Bruggen, Coosje van. *Frank O. Gehry: Guggenheim Museum Bilbao.* New York: Guggenheim Museum, 1999.

Isenberg, Barbara. *Conversations with Frank Gehry.* New York: Alfred A. Knopf, 2009.

Ragheb, J. Fiona, ed. *Frank Gehry, Architect.* New York: Guggenheim Museum, 2001.

Sketches of Frank Gehry. Directed by Sydney Pollack. Culver City, CA: Sony Pictures Home Entertainment. Released August 22, 2006. DVD, 83 min.

QUOTATION SOURCES

Thangavelu: "If they . . . build it." Quoted in Bob Calverly, "Living and Working on Mars." NASA Far West Regional Technology Transfer Center. http://www.usc.edu/dept/engineering/TTC/NASA/newsarchives/may99_mars.html.

Wright: "That early . . . the world." Quoted in "Influence of Friedrich Froebel: Frank Lloyd Wright." Froebel Web. http://www.froebelweb.org/web2000.html.

Pelli: "The desire . . . human psyche." Quoted in "Cesar Pelli." Quote Times. http://www.quotetimes.com/tag/2671/Cesar-Pelli.

Fathy: "The human . . . precious resource." Hassan Fathy, *Architecture for the Poor: An Experiment in Rural Egypt* (Chicago: University of Chicago Press, 1973), xii.

Lin: "The process . . . it's magical." Quoted in "Seeing the World Differently: Maya Lin Interview." Academy of Achievement, June 16, 2000. http://www.achievement.org/autodoc/page/lin0int-2.

Tange: "Architecture must . . . human heart." Kenzo Tange, "Ceremony Acceptance Speech." The Pritzker Architecture Prize. http://www.pritzkerprize.com/1987/ceremony_speech1.

Wright: "The maple . . . this day. " Quoted in "Frank Lloyd Wright, Architect (1867–1959)." Design Museum. http://designmuseum.org/design/frank-lloyd-wright.

Gaudí: "There are . . . in nature." Quoted in "Art: Fantastic Catalan." *TIME* LIX, no. 4, Jan. 28, 1952. http://www.time.com/time/magazine/article/0,9171,806302,00.html.

Safdie: "I want . . . their own." Quoted in "Man's Basic Needs." Oracle ThinkQuest Education Foundation. http://library.thinkquest.org/C0115965/english/info/solu/needs.htm.

Hadid: "In every . . . conquered." Quoted in Yehuda Safran, "Planet Zaha Hadid and Eduardo Souto de Moura." Prototypo Essays 003. http://www.prototypo.com/Essays/Essays3/003_3.htm.

Fuller: "[Children] spontaneously . . . experiences." Quoted in "Quotations by the Author: R. Buckminster Fuller (1895–1983)." The Quotations Page. http://www.quotationspage.com/quotes/R._Buckminster_Fuller.

Vélez: "Bamboo is . . . of nature." Quoted in "Bamboo magic: Colombian architect works wonders with 'green steel.'" *Sunday Hindustan Times,* Sept. 5, 2004. http://www.bambootech.org/tslink.asp?subsubid=71&subid=16&sname=MISSION&lid=21.Document2.

Khalili: "Everything we . . . the place." Quoted in Brian Ackley, "The Adventures of Super Adobe." *Tavoos Art Magazine.* http://www.tavoosonline.com/Articles/ArticleDetailEn.aspx?src=126&Page=2.

Ban: "Anything can . . . structure material." Quoted in Martin Moeller, "The Art of Building Lightly: An Interview with Shigeru Ban." National Building Museum. http://www.nbm.org/about-us/publications/blueprints/the-art-of-building-lightly.html.

Adjaye: "Space is . . . fill it." Quoted in interview with Diego Garcia Scaro. *IconEye: Icon Magazine Online.* http://www.iconeye.com/news/david-adjaye.

Gehry: "Creativity is . . . your intuition." Quoted in "Frank Gehry Art Quotes." The Painter's Keys. http://quote.robertgenn.com/auth_search.php?authid=562.